D0423141

Property of
Louisville Public Library

CARYL CHURCHILL

Caryl Churchill has written for the stage, television and radio. Her stage plays include *Owners* (Royal Court Theatre Upstairs, 1972); *Objections to Sex and Violence* (Royal Court, 1975); *Light Shining in Buckinghamshire* (Joint Stock on tour incl. Theatre Upstairs, 1976); *Vinegar Tom* (Monstrous Regiment on tour, incl. Half Moon and ICA, 1976); *Traps* (Theatre Upstairs, 1977), *Cloud Nine* (Joint Stock on tour incl. Royal Court, London, 1979, then Theatre de Lys, New York, 1981); *Three More Sleepless Nights* (Soho Poly and Theatre Upstairs, 1980); *Top Girls* (Royal Court, London, then Public Theatre, New York, 1982); *Fen* (Joint Stock on tour, incl. Almeida and Royal Court, London, then Public Theatre, New York, 1983); *Softcops* (RSC at the Pit, 1984); *A Mouthful of Birds* with David Lan (Joint Stock on tour, incl. Royal Court, 1986); *Serious Money* (Royal Court and Wyndham's, London, then Public Theatre, New York, 1987); *Icecream* (Royal Court, 1989); *Mad Forest* (Central School of Speech and Drama, then Royal Court, 1990); *Lives of the Great Poisoners* with Orlando Gough and Ian Spink (Second Stride on tour, incl. Riverside Studios, London, 1991); *The Skriker* (Royal National Theatre, 1994); *Thyestes* translated from Seneca (Royal Court Theatre Upstairs, 1994); *Hotel* with Orlando Gough and Ian Spink (Second Stride on tour, incl. The Place, London, 1997); *This is a Chair* (London International Festival of Theatre at the Royal Court, 1997); *Blue Heart* (Joint Stock on tour, incl. Royal Court Theatre, 1997); *Far Away* (Royal Court Theatre Upstairs, 2000, then Albery, London 2001).

Other works by the same author in this series

Light Shining in Buckinghamshire (TCG)
Traps
Cloud Nine (TCG)
Icecream
Mad Forest (TCG)
The Skriker (TCG)
Thyestes (translated from Seneca)
Hotel
This is a Chair
Blue Heart (TCG)

Collections

Shorts
- *Lovesick*
- *Abortive*
- *Not Not Not Not Not Enough Oxygen*
- *Schreber's Nervous Illness*
- *The Hospital at the Time of the Revolution*
- *The Judge's Wife*
- *The After-Dinner Joke*
- *Seagulls*
- *Three More Sleepless Nights*
- *Hot Fudge*

Plays: Three
- *A Mouthful of Birds* (co-author: David Lan)
- *Icecream*
- *Mad Forest*
- *Lives of the Great Poisoners* (co-authors Orlando Gough and Ian Spink)
- *The Skriker*
- *Thyestes* (translated from Seneca)

CARYL CHURCHILL

Far Away

THEATRE
COMMUNICATIONS
GROUP

New York

822.914
CHU

A Nick Hern Book

Far Away is published by Theatre Communications Group, Inc., 355 Lexington Ave., New York, NY 10017–6603, by special arrangement with Nick Hern Books Limited

Far Away first published in 2000 as a paperback original by Nick Hern Books, 14 Larden Road, London W3 7ST in association with the Royal Court Theatre

Far Away copyright © 2000 by Caryl Churchill Ltd

Caryl Churchill has asserted her right to be identified as the author of this work

Cover design: Ned Hoste, 2H

Typeset by Country Setting, Kingsdown, Kent, CT14 8ES
Printed and bound in Mexico

ISBN 0-7394-3181-1

Amateur Performing Rights Applications for performance in excerpt or in full by non-professionals in English throughout the world should be addressed to Samuel French Inc., 45 West 25th Street, NY 10010 (*phone* 212-206-1429) or their overseas agents.

Publication of the play does not necessarily indicate its availability for amateur performance.

Professional Performing Rights Applications for performance by professionals in any medium and in any language throughout the world should be addressed to Casarotto Ramsay Ltd, National House, 60-66 Wardour Street, London, England, W1V 3HP.

No performance of any kind may be given unless a license has been obtained. Application should be made before rehearsals begin.

First TCG Edition May 2001

Far Away was first performed at the Royal Court Theatre Upstairs, London, on 24 November 2000, before transferring to the Albery Theatre in the West End on 18 January 2001. The cast was as follows:

YOUNG JOAN	Annabelle Seymour-Julen
HARPER	Linda Bassett
TODD	Kevin McKidd
OLDER JOAN	Katherine Tozer

Director Stephen Daldry
Designer Ian MacNeil
Lighting Designer Rick Fisher
Sound Designer Paul Arditti

FAR AWAY

Characters

JOAN, *a girl*

HARPER, *her aunt*

TODD, *a young man*

The Parade (Scene 2.5): five is too few and twenty better than ten. A hundred?

1.

HARPER*'s house. Night.*

JOAN I can't sleep.

HARPER It's the strange bed.

JOAN No, I like different places.

HARPER Are you cold?

JOAN No.

HARPER Do you want a drink?

JOAN I think I am cold.

HARPER That's easy enough then. There's extra blankets in the cupboard.

JOAN Is it late?

HARPER Two.

JOAN Are you going to bed?

HARPER Do you want a hot drink?

JOAN No thank you.

HARPER I should go to bed then.

JOAN Yes.

HARPER It's always odd in a new place. When you've been here a week you'll look back at tonight and it won't seem the same at all.

JOAN I've been to a lot of places. I've stayed with friends at their houses. I don't miss my parents if you think that.

HARPER Do you miss your dog?

JOAN I miss the cat I think.

HARPER Does it sleep on your bed?

JOAN No because I chase it off. But it gets in if the door's not properly shut. You think you've shut the door but it hasn't caught and she pushes it open in the night.

HARPER Come here a minute. You're shivering. Are you hot?

JOAN No, I'm all right.

HARPER You're over-tired. Go to bed. I'm going to bed myself.

JOAN I went out.

HARPER When? just now?

JOAN Just now.

HARPER No wonder you're cold. It's hot in the daytime here but it's cold at night.

JOAN The stars are brighter here than at home.

HARPER It's because there's no street lights.

JOAN I couldn't see much.

HARPER I don't expect you could. How did you get out? I didn't hear the door.

JOAN I went out the window.

HARPER I'm not sure I like that.

JOAN No it's quite safe, there's a roof and a tree.

HARPER When people go to bed they should stay in bed. Do you climb out of the window at home?

JOAN I can't at home because - No I don't.

HARPER I'm responsible for you.

JOAN Yes, I'm sorry.

HARPER Well that's enough adventures for one night. You'll sleep now. Off you go. Look at you, you're asleep on your feet.

JOAN There was a reason.

HARPER For going out?

JOAN I heard a noise.

HARPER An owl?

JOAN A shriek.

HARPER An owl then. There are all sorts of birds here, you might see a golden oriole. People come here specially to watch birds and we sometimes make tea or coffee or sell bottles of water because there's no café and people don't expect that and they get thirsty. You'll see in the morning what a beautiful place it is.

JOAN It was more like a person screaming.

HARPER It is like a person screaming when you hear an owl.

JOAN It was a person screaming.

HARPER Poor girl, what a fright you must have had imagining you heard somebody screaming. You should have come straight down here to me.

JOAN I wanted to see.

HARPER It was dark.

JOAN Yes but I did see.

HARPER Now what did you imagine you saw in the dark?

JOAN I saw my uncle.

HARPER Yes I expect you did. He likes a breath of air. He wasn't screaming I hope?

JOAN No.

HARPER That's all right then. Did you talk to him? I expect you were frightened he'd say what are you doing out of your bed so late.

JOAN I stayed in the tree.

HARPER He didn't see you?

JOAN No.

HARPER He'll be surprised won't he, he'll laugh when he hears you were up in the tree. He'll be cross but he doesn't mean it, he'll think it's a good joke, it's the sort of thing he did when he was a boy. So bed now. I'll go up too.

JOAN He was pushing someone. He was bundling someone into a shed.

HARPER He must have been putting a big sack in the shed. He works too late.

JOAN I'm not sure if it was a woman. It could have been a young man.

HARPER Well I have to tell you, when you've been married as long as I have. There are things people get up to, it's natural, it's nothing bad, that's just friends of his your uncle was having a little party with.

JOAN Was it a party?

HARPER Just a little party.

JOAN Yes because there wasn't just that one person.

HARPER No, there'd be a few of his friends.

JOAN There was a lorry.

HARPER Yes, I expect there was.

JOAN When I put my ear against the side of the lorry I heard crying inside.

HARPER How could you do that from up in the tree?

JOAN I got down from the tree. I went to the lorry after I looked in the window of the shed.

HARPER There might be things that are not your business when you're a visitor in someone else's house.

JOAN Yes, I'd rather not have seen. I'm sorry.

HARPER Nobody saw you?

JOAN They were thinking about themselves.

HARPER I think it's lucky nobody saw you.

JOAN If it's a party, why was there so much blood?

HARPER There isn't any blood.

JOAN Yes.

HARPER Where?

JOAN On the ground.

HARPER In the dark? how would you see that in the dark?

JOAN I slipped in it.

She holds up her bare foot.

I mostly wiped it off.

HARPER That's where the dog got run over this afternoon.

JOAN Wouldn't it have dried up?

HARPER Not if the ground was muddy.

JOAN What sort of dog?

HARPER A big dog, a big mongrel.

JOAN That's awful, you must be very sad, had you had him long?

HARPER No, he was young, he ran out, he was never very obedient, a lorry was backing up.

JOAN What was his name?

HARPER Flash.

JOAN What colour was he?

HARPER Black with a bit of white.

JOAN Why were the children in the shed?

HARPER What children?

JOAN Don't you know what children?

HARPER How could you see there were children?

JOAN There was a light on. That's how I could see the blood inside the shed. I could see the faces and which ones had blood on.

HARPER You've found out something secret. You know that don't you?

JOAN Yes.

HARPER Something you shouldn't know.

JOAN Yes I'm sorry.

HARPER Something you must never talk about. Because if you do you could put people's lives in danger.

JOAN Why? who from? from my uncle?

HARPER Of course not from your uncle.

JOAN From you?

HARPER Of course not from me, are you mad? I'm going to tell you what's going on. Your uncle is helping these people. He's helping them escape. He's giving them shelter. Some of them were still in the lorry, that's why they were crying. Your uncle's going to take them all into the shed and then they'll be all right.

JOAN They had blood on their faces.

HARPER That's from before. That's because they were attacked by the people your uncle's saving them from.

JOAN There was blood on the ground.

HARPER One of them was injured very badly but your uncle bandaged him up.

JOAN He's helping them.

HARPER That's right.

JOAN There wasn't a dog. There wasn't a party.

HARPER No, I'm trusting you with the truth now. You must never talk about it or you'll put your uncle's life in danger and mine and even your own. You won't even say anything to your parents.

JOAN Why did you have me to stay if you've got this secret going on?

HARPER The lorry should have come yesterday. It won't happen again while you're here.

JOAN It can now because I know. You don't have to stop for me. I could help uncle in the shed and look after them.

HARPER No, he has to do it himself. But thank you for offering, that's very kind. So after all that excitement do you think you could go back to bed?

JOAN Why was uncle hitting them?

HARPER Hitting who?

JOAN He was hitting a man with a stick. I think the stick was metal. He hit one of the children.

HARPER One of the people in the lorry was a traitor. He wasn't really one of them, he was pretending, he was going to betray them, they found out and told your uncle. Then he attacked your uncle, he attacked the other people, your uncle had to fight him.

JOAN That's why there was so much blood.

HARPER Yes, it had to be done to save the others.

JOAN He hit one of the children.

HARPER That would have been the child of the traitor. Or sometimes you get bad children who even betray their parents.

JOAN What's going to happen?

HARPER They'll go off in the lorry very early in the morning.

JOAN Where to?

HARPER Where they're escaping to. You don't want to have to keep any more secrets.

JOAN He only hit the traitors.

HARPER Of course. I'm not surprised you can't sleep, what an upsetting thing to see. But now you understand, it's not so bad. You're part of a big movement now to make things better. You can be proud of that. You can look at the stars and think here we are in our little bit of space, and I'm on the side of the people who are putting things right, and your soul will expand right into the sky.

JOAN Can't I help?

HARPER You can help me clean up in the morning. Will you do that?

JOAN Yes.

HARPER So you'd better get some sleep.

2.

Several years later. A hat makers.

1.

JOAN *and* TODD *are sitting at a workbench. They have each just started making a hat.*

TODD There's plenty of blue.

JOAN I think I'm starting with black.

TODD Colour always wins.

JOAN I will have colour, I'm starting with black to set the colour off.

TODD I did one last week that was an abstract picture of the street, blue for the buses, yellow for the flats, red for the leaves, grey for the sky. Nobody got it but I knew what it was. There's little satisfactions to be had.

JOAN Don't you enjoy it?

TODD You're new aren't you?

JOAN This is my first hat. My first professional hat.

TODD Did you do hat at college?

JOAN My degree hat was a giraffe six feet tall.

TODD You won't have time to do something like that in the week.

JOAN I know.

TODD We used to get two weeks before a parade and then they took it down to one and now they're talking about cutting a day.

JOAN So we'd get an extra day off?

TODD We'd get a day's less money. We wouldn't make such good hats.

JOAN Can they do that?

TODD You'd oppose it would you?

JOAN I've only just started.

TODD You'll find there's a lot wrong with this place.

JOAN I thought it was one of the best jobs.

TODD It is. Do you know where to go for lunch?

JOAN I think there's a canteen isn't there?

TODD Yes but we don't go there. I'll show you where to go.

2.

Next day. They are working on the hats, which are by now far more brightly decorated ie the ones they were working on have been replaced by ones nearer completion.

JOAN Your turn.

TODD I go for a swim in the river before work.

JOAN Isn't it dangerous?

TODD Your turn.

JOAN I've got a pilot's licence.

TODD I stay up till four every morning watching the trials.

JOAN I'm getting a room in a subway.

TODD I've got my own place.

JOAN Have you?

TODD Do you want to see it? That's coming on.

JOAN I don't understand yours but I like the feather.

TODD I'm not trying. I've been here too long.

JOAN Will you leave?

TODD My turn. There's something wrong with how we get the contracts.

JOAN But we want the contracts.

TODD What if we don't deserve them? What if our work isn't really the best?

JOAN So what's going on?

TODD I'll just say a certain person's brother-in-law. Where does he work do you think?

JOAN Where does he work?

TODD I'm not talking about it in here. Tell me something else.

JOAN I don't like staying in in the evenings and watching trials.

TODD I watch them at night after I come back.

JOAN Back from where?

TODD Where do you like?

3.

Next day. They're working on the hats, which are getting very big and extravagant.

TODD I don't enjoy animal hats myself.

JOAN I was a student.

TODD Abstract hats are back in a big way.

JOAN I've always liked abstract hats.

TODD You must have not noticed when everyone hated them.

JOAN It was probably before my time.

Silence. They go on working.

JOAN It's just if you're going on about it all the time I don't know why you don't do something about it.

TODD This is your third day.

JOAN The management's corrupt – you've told me. We're too low paid – you've told me.

Silence. They go on working.

TODD Too much green.

JOAN It's meant to be too much.

Silence. They go on working.

TODD I noticed you looking at that fair boy's hat. I hope you told him it was derivative.

Silence. They go on working.

TODD I'm the only person in this place who's got any principles, don't tell me I should do something, I spend my days wondering what to do.

JOAN So you'll probably come up with something.

Silence. They go on working.

4.

Next day. They are working on the hats, which are now enormous and preposterous.

TODD That's beautiful.

JOAN You like it?

TODD I do.

JOAN I like yours too.

TODD You don't have to say that. It's not one of my best.

JOAN No it's got - I don't know, it's a confident hat.

TODD I have been doing parades for six years. So I'm a valued old hand. So when I go and speak to a certain person he might pay attention.

JOAN You're going to speak to him?

TODD I've an appointment after work.

JOAN You might lose your job.

TODD I might.

JOAN I'm impressed.

TODD That was the idea.

JOAN Will you mention the brother-in-law?

TODD First I'll talk about the money. Then I'll just touch in the brother-in-law. I've a friend who's a journalist.

JOAN Will you touch in the journalist?

TODD I might imply something without giving the journalist away. It might be better if he can't trace the journalist back to me.

JOAN Though he will suspect.

TODD However much he suspects. One thing if I lost my job.

JOAN What's that?

TODD I'd miss you.

JOAN Already?

5.

Next day. A procession of ragged, beaten, chained prisoners, each wearing a hat, on their way to execution. The finished hats are even more enormous and preposterous than in the previous scene.

6.

A new week. JOAN *and* TODD *are starting work on new hats.*

JOAN I still can't believe it.

TODD No one's ever won in their first week before.

JOAN It's all going to be downhill from now on.

TODD You can't win every week.

JOAN That's what I mean.

TODD No but you'll do a fantastic body of work while you're here.

JOAN Sometimes I think it's a pity that more aren't kept.

TODD There'd be too many, what would they do with them?

JOAN They could reuse them.

TODD Exactly and then we'd be out of work.

JOAN It seems so sad to burn them with the bodies.

TODD No I think that's the joy of it. The hats are ephemeral. It's like a metaphor for something or other.

JOAN Well, life.

TODD Well, life, there you are. Out of nearly three hundred hats I've made here I've only had three win and go in the museum. But that's never bothered me. You make beauty and it disappears, I love that.

JOAN You're so..

TODD What?

JOAN You make me think in different ways. Like I'd never have thought about how this place is run and now I see how important it is.

TODD I think it did impress a certain person that I was speaking from the high moral ground.

JOAN So tell me again exactly what he said at the end.

TODD "These things must be thought about."

JOAN I think that's encouraging.

TODD It could mean he'll think how to get rid of me.

JOAN That's a fantastic shape to start from.

TODD It's a new one for me. I'm getting inspired by you.

JOAN There's still the journalist. If he looks into it a bit more we could expose the corrupt financial basis of how the whole hat industry is run, not just this place, I bet the whole industry is dodgy.

TODD Do you think so?

JOAN I think we should find out.

TODD You've changed my life, do you know that?

JOAN If you lose your job I'll resign.

TODD We might not get jobs in hats again.

JOAN There's other parades.

TODD But I think you're a hat genius.

JOAN Unless all the parades are corrupt.

TODD I love these beads. Use these beads.

JOAN No, you have them.

TODD No, you.

3.

Several years later. HARPER*'s house, daytime.*

HARPER You were right to poison the wasps.

TODD Yes, I think all the wasps have got to go.

HARPER I was outside yesterday on the edge of the wood when a shadow came over and it was a cloud of butterflies, and they came down just beyond me and the trees and bushes were red with them. Two of them clung to my arm, I was terrified, one of them got in my hair, I managed to squash them.

TODD I haven't had a problem with butterflies.

HARPER They can cover your face. The Romans used to commit suicide with gold leaf, just flip it down their throat and it covered their windpipe, I think of that with butterflies.

TODD I was passing an orchard, there were horses standing under the trees, and suddenly wasps attacked them out of the plums. There were the horses galloping by screaming with their heads made of wasp. I wish she'd wake up.

HARPER We don't know how long she'd been walking.

TODD She was right to come.

HARPER You don't go walking off in the middle of a war.

TODD You do if you're escaping.

HARPER We don't know that she was escaping.

TODD She was getting to a place of safety to regroup.

HARPER Is this a place of safety?

TODD Relatively, yes of course it is. Everyone thinks it's just a house.

HARPER The cats have come in on the side of the French.

TODD I never liked cats, they smell, they scratch, they only like you because you feed them, they bite, I used to have a cat that would suddenly just take some bit of you in its mouth.

HARPER Did you know they've been killing babies?

TODD Where's that?

HARPER In China. They jump in the cots when nobody's looking.

TODD But some cats are still ok.

HARPER I don't think so.

TODD I know a cat up the road.

HARPER No, you must be careful of that.

TODD But we're not exactly on the other side from the French. It's not as if they're the Moroccans and the ants.

HARPER It's not as if they're the Canadians, the Venezuelans and the mosquitoes.

TODD It's not as if they're the engineers, the chefs, the children under five, the musicians.

HARPER The car salesmen.

TODD Portuguese car salesmen.

HARPER Russian swimmers.

TODD Thai butchers.

HARPER Latvian dentists.

TODD No, the Latvian dentists have been doing good work in Cuba. They've a house outside Havana.

HARPER But Latvia has been sending pigs to Sweden. The dentists are linked to international dentistry and that's where their loyalty lies, with dentists in Dar-es-Salaam.

TODD We don't argue about Dar-es-Salaam.

HARPER You would attempt to justify the massacre in Dar-es-Salaam?

She's come here because you're here on leave and if anyone finds out I'll be held responsible.

TODD It's only till tomorrow. I'll wake her up. I'll give her a few more minutes.

HARPER Did you see the programme about crocodiles?

TODD Yes but crocodiles, the way they look after the baby crocodiles and carry them down to the water in their mouths.

HARPER Don't you think everyone helps their own children?

TODD I'm just saying I wouldn't be sorry if the crocodiles were on one of the sides we have alliances with. They're unstoppable, come on.

HARPER Crocodiles are evil and it is always right to be opposed to crocodiles. Their skin, their teeth, the foul smell of their mouths from the dead meat. Crocodiles wait till zebras are crossing the river and bite the weak ones with those jaws and pull them down. Crocodiles invade villages at night and take children out of their beds. A crocodile will carry a dozen heads back to the river, tenderly like it carries its young, and put them in the water where they bob about as trophies till they rot.

TODD I'm just saying we could use that.

HARPER And the fluffy little darling waterbirds, the smallest one left behind squeaking wait for me, wait for me. And their mother who would give her life to save them.

TODD Do we include mallards in this?

HARPER Mallards are not a good waterbird. They commit rape, and they're on the side of the elephants and the Koreans. But crocodiles are always in the wrong.

TODD Do you think I should wake her up or let her sleep? We won't get any time together.

HARPER You agree with me about the crocodiles?

TODD What's the matter? you don't know whose side I'm on?

HARPER I don't know what you think.

TODD I think what we all think.

HARPER Take deer.

TODD You mean sweet little bambis?

HARPER You mean that ironically?

TODD I mean it sarcastically.

HARPER Because they burst out of parks and storm down from mountains and terrorise shopping malls. If the does run away when you shoot they run into

somebody else and trample them with their vicious little shining hooves, the fawns get under the feet of shoppers and send them crashing down escalators, the young bucks charge the plate glass windows –

TODD I know to hate deer.

HARPER and the old ones, do you know how heavy their antlers are or how sharp the prongs are when they twist into teenagers running down the street?

TODD Yes I do know that.

He lifts his shirt and shows a scar.

HARPER Was that a deer?

TODD In fact it was a bear. I don't like being doubted.

HARPER It was when the elephants went over to the Dutch, I'd always trusted elephants.

TODD I've shot cattle and children in Ethiopia. I've gassed mixed troops of Spanish, computer programmers and dogs. I've torn starlings apart with my bare hands. And I liked doing it with my bare hands. So don't suggest I'm not reliable.

HARPER I'm not saying you can't kill.

TODD And I know it's not all about excitement. I've done boring jobs. I've worked in abattoirs stunning pigs and musicians and by the end of the day your back aches and all you can see when you shut your eyes is people hanging upside down by their feet.

HARPER So you'd say the deer are vicious?

TODD We've been over that.

HARPER If a hungry deer came into the yard you wouldn't feed it?

TODD Of course not.

HARPER I don't understand that because the deer are with us. They have been for three weeks.

TODD I didn't know. You said yourself.

HARPER Their natural goodness has come through. You can see it in their soft brown eyes.

TODD That's good news.

HARPER You hate the deer. You admire the crocodiles.

TODD I've lost touch because I'm tired.

HARPER You must leave.

TODD I'm your family.

HARPER Do you think I sleep?

JOAN *comes in and walks into* TODD*'s arms.*

HARPER You can't stay here, they'll be after you. What are you going to say when you go back, you ran off to spend a day with your husband? Everyone has people they love they'd like to see or anyway people they'd rather see than lie in a hollow waiting to be bitten by ants. Are you not going back at all because if you're not you might as well shoot me now. Did anyone see you leave? which way did you come? were you followed? There are ospreys here who will have seen you arrive. And you're risking your life for you don't know what because he says things that aren't right. Don't you care? Maybe you don't know right from wrong yourself, what do I know about you after two years, I'd like to be glad to see you but how can I?

JOAN Of course birds saw me, everyone saw me walking along but nobody knew why, I could have been on a mission, everyone's moving about and no one knows why, and in fact I killed two cats and a child under five so it wasn't that different from a mission, and I don't see why I can't have one day and then go back, I'll go on to the end after this. It wasn't so much the birds I was frightened of, it was the weather, the weather here's on the side of the Japanese. There were thunderstorms all through the mountains, I went through towns I hadn't been before. The rats are bleeding out of their mouths and ears, which is good, and so were the girls by the side of the road. It was tiring there because everything's been recruited, there were piles of bodies and if you stopped to find out there was one killed by coffee or one killed by pins, they were killed by heroin, petrol, chainsaws, hairspray, bleach, foxgloves, the smell of smoke was where we were burning the grass that wouldn't serve. The Bolivians are working with gravity, that's a secret so as not to spread alarm. But we're getting further with noise and there's thousands dead of light in Madagascar. Who's going to mobilise darkness and silence? that's what I wondered in the night. By the third day I could hardly walk but I got down to the river. There was a camp of Chilean soldiers upstream but they hadn't seen me and fourteen black and white cows downstream having a drink so I knew I'd have to go straight across. But I didn't know whose side the river was on, it might help me swim or it might drown me. In the middle the current was running much faster, the water was brown, I didn't know if that meant anything. I stood on the bank a long time. But I knew it was my only way of getting here so at last I put one foot in the river. It was very cold but so far that was all. When you've just stepped in you can't tell what's going to happen. The water laps round your ankles in any case.

Francis McDormand as Harper. All photographs from the New York Theatre Workshop production of *Far Away*. © Joan Marcus.

Francis McDormand as Harper and Alexa Eisenstein as Joan as a child. © Joan Marcus.

Marin Ireland as Joan and Chris Messina as Todd. © Joan Marcus.

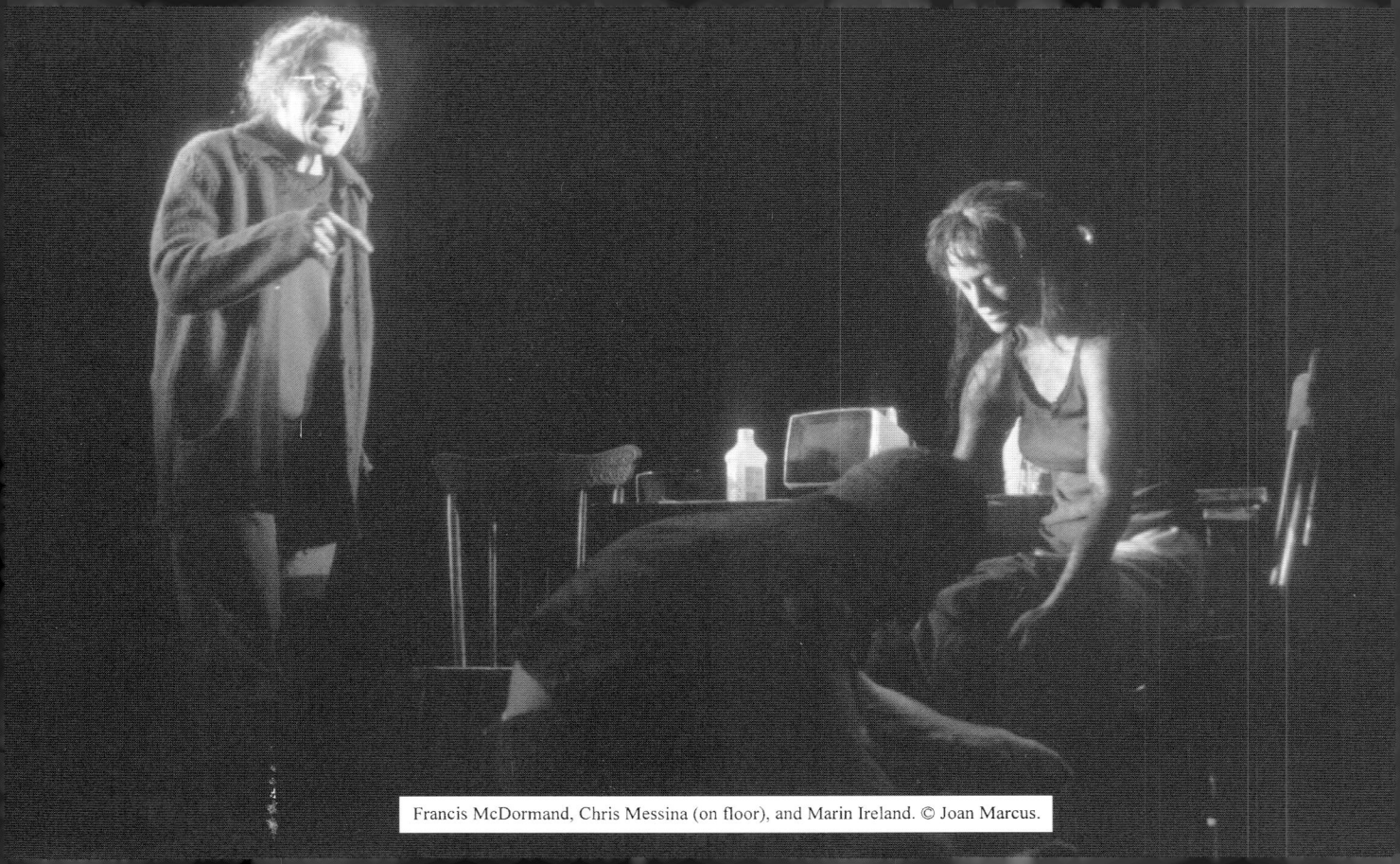

Francis McDormand, Chris Messina (on floor), and Marin Ireland. © Joan Marcus.